Best of the West Biographies

Billy the Kid
Wild West Outlaw

Elaine Landau

E **Enslow Publishers, Inc.**

40 Industrial Road	PO Box 38
Box 398	Aldershot
Berkeley Heights, NJ 07922	Hants GU12 6BP
USA	UK

http://www.enslow.com

Library of Congress Cataloging-in-Publication Data

Landau, Elaine.
   Billy the Kid : wild west outlaw / Elaine Landau.
     p. cm. — (Best of the West biographies)
   Summary: A biography of Billy, the Kid, an outlaw of the Old West, from his childhood and participation in the Lincoln County Range War to his death at the hands of Pat Garrett.
   Includes bibliographical references and index.
   ISBN 0-7660-2207-2 (hardcover)
   1. Billy, the Kid—Juvenile literature. 2. Outlaws—Southwest, New—Biography—Juvenile literature. 3. Southwest, New—Biography—Juvenile literature. [1. Billy, the Kid. 2. Robbers and outlaws.] I. Title. II. Series.
F786.B54L36 2004
364.15'52'092—dc21
                                    2003010333

Printed in the United States of America

10 9 8 7 6 5 4 3 2 1

To Our Readers: We have done our best to make sure that all Internet addresses in this book were active and appropriate when we went to press. However, the author and publisher have no control over and assume no liability for the material available on those Internet sites or on other Web sites they may link to. Any comments or suggestions can be sent by e-mail to comments@enslow.com or to the address on the back cover.

Contents

Billy the Kid

A Small Outlaw

The Year: 1875

The Place: Silver City, New Mexico

Sheriff Harvey Whitehall was upset. He had a difficult teenager on his hands. The youth was Henry McCarty. Henry was fifteen. Yet the blue-eyed, blondish boy looked much younger. Henry was short and slimly built. He often passed for twelve.

Most people liked being around McCarty. He could be a lot of fun. However, that did not include Sheriff Whitehall. Whitehall was Silver City's top lawman. Lately, he had been seeing too much of Henry McCarty.

In the past, Henry had been law abiding. He read a lot and liked music. Most days, he

The game of pool is played by "shooting" fifteen numbered balls into pockets in a table with pool sticks called "cues."

helped his teacher after school. Unlike some boys, he never swore.

Then Henry began to change. There might have been a good reason for it. His mother died. Catherine McCarty had been ill for a long time. She had a lung disease called tuberculosis. Henry was not close to his stepfather. He had never been much of a parent to him.

The teen started to skip school. Henry spent hours in the pool hall. Before long he got into trouble. First Henry stole several pounds of butter from a rancher. He tried to sell it to a local merchant. Sheriff Whitehall was promptly called.

Henry's new friend, George Shaffer, made things worse. George was also known as Sombrero Jack because of his large Mexican-style hat. George loved that hat. It was about the only thing he had that had not been not stolen.

George taught Henry to steal. They sometimes worked together. But usually only Henry was the one who got caught.

That happened when the boys stole some clothes. They took the items from the town's Chinese laundry. Sombrero Jack did not take the goods with him. He told Henry to hide them instead. Once again, Henry got caught. By then, Sombrero Jack was nowhere to be found.

Sombreros are wide-brimmed, hats. They are sometimes decorated.

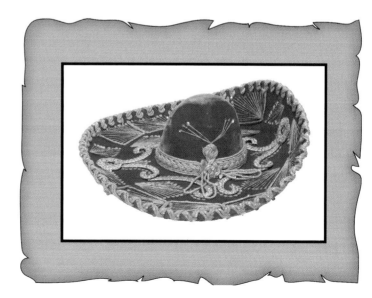

Sheriff Whitehall did not know what to do with Henry. He had spoken to him before. Once he even spanked him. Nothing seemed to work. So, Whitehall tried something harsher. He took Henry to jail. The Sheriff did not put Henry in a cell. The boy seemed too young for that. Instead, he placed a cot in the hallway for him.

Later on, the Sheriff went out. He locked the door to the jail. Whitehall came back about a half

Jail cells in the 1870s were very different from the ones we have today. Usually, prisoners were locked in one large room, and there was only one guard at a time to watch them.

hour later. Henry was gone. The boy had found a way out. He climbed up the chimney. Henry was small enough to push his way through. Then he jumped from the roof to freedom.

Henry had to leave town. He did not want to see Sheriff Whitehall again. This time he might end up in a locked cell. He set off on his own. Some thought he was fearless. Others thought he was just foolish. They were probably right on both counts.

Henry was young to be on his own. Much of the West was still wild and unsettled. Breaking out of jail had been a bad idea too. At fifteen, Henry McCarty had become an outlaw. Yet he was really just a kid. People would see that. He would soon be known as Billy the Kid.

Henry McCarty was known by other names such as William H. Bonney, but he was best known as Billy the Kid.

On to Arizona

Henry McCarthy left New Mexico in a hurry. There was no time to pack. He did not even say goodbye to his friends. Henry just headed west for Arizona. That was a long way from where his life had begun. Henry was born in New York City. His birth date was probably November 23, 1859.

Not much is known about Henry's early years. His mother, Catherine McCarty, came to America from Ireland. She had one other son named Joseph. Joseph might have been older or younger than Henry. No one is sure.

Even less is known about Henry's father.

However, his mother married his stepfather in 1873. She met him after moving West with her sons.

Leaving Silver City was hard for Henry. He had never had much of a family. Now he left everyone he knew behind. Henry needed a place to stay. He needed a job too. He found both in Arizona at the Hooker Ranch. There, Henry roped cattle and tended horses. He also did repairs.

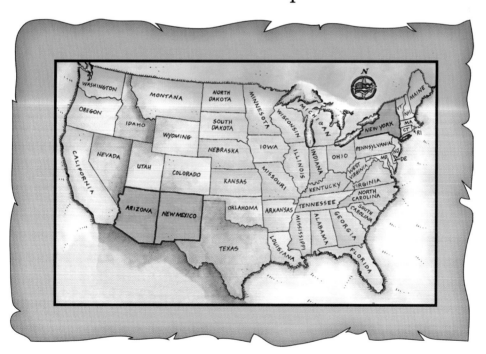

Traveling great distances, such as from New York to New Mexico or from New Mexico to Arizona, was not easy in the 1800s. Many people traveled on horseback, in carriages, stagecoaches, or on much slower trains than we have today.

Roping calves is a difficult job that requires a lot of skill.

But Henry was not there very long. He was still just a boy. Henry was not strong enough to do the job well. Before long, he was fired.

At that point, Henry started stealing again. His new friends were thieves. Sometimes they stole small items. Other times they stole horses. Horse stealing was serious. There were no cars at the time. People needed their horses to get around.

At first Henry was not caught. But that changed soon enough. One night, Henry stole the wrong horse. The animal belonged to Sergeant Lewis C. Hartman. Hartman was a United States cavalry officer. He was not about to lose his favorite horse.

Hartman gathered a small group of soldiers. They set out to find the horse thief. The trail led straight to Henry.

The cavalry were members of the military who fought on horseback.

The sergeant took back his horse. But that was not the worst of it. He also reported the crime to the law. Henry was arrested for horse stealing and taken to jail.

He would not be there long, though. As before, Henry was determined to escape.

This time, he did not leave through the chimney. Instead, Henry hid a handful of salt from dinner. When only one guard was on duty, he threw the salt in the guard's eyes. Then, the teen made a run for it. He did not get very far. Two other guards were still outside. They caught Henry and brought him back.

The teen was put in irons. That made the sheriff feel better. He thought that Henry was there to stay. He was wrong. Later that night, Henry escaped again. No one was sure how he did it. But both the boy and the irons were gone.

The townspeople were amazed. They told the story over and over. It always ended the same way. People simply said, "The kid is gone!"

Henry McCarty soon became known as The Kid. The label fit the small teenager well.

Even iron cuffs did not keep Henry from escaping.

After a while, Henry took the name Billy. Before long, everyone started calling him Billy the Kid. The name stuck.

Billy the Kid had been in trouble for stealing. But he had never killed a man. That is, until the summer of 1877. One evening that August, Billy went to a saloon. A blacksmith named Windy Cahill was there too. Windy was a large man. He was also a bully who often picked on Billy.

Windy would tease Billy about being small. Sometimes, he pushed or slapped him. Other times,

Windy ruffled Billy's hair. He did this in front of the other men. Windy liked to embarrass Billy.

But that night, Billy fought back. He called Windy a name. Punches were thrown. The men wrestled on the floor. Windy was more than twice Billy's size. The Kid did not have a chance.

Saloons were places for men to talk, drink, and play cards. Sometimes the card games ended in violence.

It looked as though Windy might kill him.

Somehow, Billy was able to pull out his pistol. Windy tried to take the gun away from him. But Billy fired first. He shot Windy in the stomach. The blacksmith died the next day.

Gun owners took pride in the fancy carvings on their pistols.

Not everyone blamed Billy. Some said he had fired in self-defense. But the law saw it differently. The Kid did not want to stand trial for murder. So, he did not wait to be arrested. Soon after the gun went off, the Kid took off as well. His days in Arizona were over.

Welcome to Lincoln County

After Arizona, Billy was not sure where to go. He thought of going to Mexico. The Kid spoke Spanish well. Billy had many Mexican friends. He had learned the language from them.

Yet instead Billy wound up in Lincoln, New Mexico. Lincoln was not much of a town. It was just one street long. There was only one two-story building. That was the general store. The store was owned by Lawrence G. Murphy and James J. Dolan. These men owned large cattle ranches in the county as well. Dolan and Murphy controlled the town's dry goods business. They also controlled the area's cattle trade. Both were powerful men who liked things as they were.

James Dolan and Lawrence Murphy
were businessmen who wanted to control
the cattle market in Lincoln County.

Lincoln was a lawless place. It had more than its share of bandits and gamblers. Fights often broke out in the saloon. Disputes were usually settled with guns. Shootouts were common in Lincoln. So were the unmarked graves of the losers.

Disagreements in the 1800s sometimes ended in gunfights.

Nevertheless, Billy the Kid felt at home there. By now, he was seventeen. He knew how to ride, shoot, and steal. He spent many

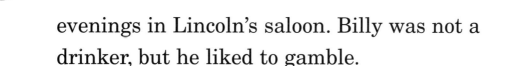
evenings in Lincoln's saloon. Billy was not a drinker, but he liked to gamble.

Billy the Kid had a number of girlfriends. He knew some of the dancehall girls at the saloon. He also met other women. Though still slim, the Kid had gotten a bit taller. Women liked his boyish charm. They enjoyed his sense of humor, too.

Billy the Kid was not afraid of danger. That was important in Lincoln. The Kid had come there at a difficult time. Trouble had been brewing in the county for months.

James J. Dolan and Lawrence G. Murphy were wealthy but dishonest businessmen. They hired rustlers or cattle thieves to steal other ranchers' cattle. Murphy and Dolan sold these cows in Mexico. They made a handsome profit. They did not want things to change.

But things changed in 1876. An Englishman named John Tunstall came to Lincoln County. Tunstall went into the cattle business. He also opened a general store. An American lawyer named Alexander McSween helped him get started.

McSween and Tunstall made a good team. Together they earned quite a bit of money. This cut into Dolan's and Murphy's profits and that made them very angry.

Two sides formed. On one side were Dolan, Murphy, and their men. The other side was made up of Tunstall, McSween, and their men. Feelings were tense in Lincoln County. It looked like the two sides might go to war.

A judge's decision sparked the fighting. In 1877, some people who had hired Alexander McSween as a lawyer were

Raising cattle was the way many people in the West, including Billy the Kid, made their living.

John Tunstall hired Billy the Kid to work for him, and the two quickly became friends.

unhappy. They claimed that McSween owed them money. A judge heard their story and agreed. McSween and Tunstall had been business partners. So, the judge ordered that part of Tunstall's cattle herd be taken to pay the debt.

The judge's decision delighted Murphy and Dolan. They wanted to drive Tunstall out of business. They hoped that lessening his herd would help. But something much worse happened.

On February 8, 1878, Sheriff William Brady headed for Tunstall's ranch to get the cattle.

He brought along some of his friends, whom he had made deputies. None of those men should have gone. All were too close to Tunstall's enemies. The new deputies worked for Dolan and Murphy. Sheriff Brady was a good friend of theirs, as well.

On their way to his ranch, the group met Tunstall on the road. They told him what they wanted. Tunstall said that the cattle were his.

The men refused to listen. Instead, they drew their guns. They ordered Tunstall to give up his weapon. Tunstall did what

After Sheriff William Brady told his deputies to kill John Tunstall, Billy the Kid vowed revenge.

they asked. He said, "I don't want any trouble." Seconds later, one of the deputies shot him. Tunstall fell to the ground. Then, another deputy shot him in the head. Tunstall died instantly.

The deputies had broken the unspoken Code of the West. They killed an unarmed man in cold blood. Once Tunstall gave up his gun, he was as good as dead. Some said the men had really come to kill Tunstall. The cattle had just been an excuse.

Billy the Kid was angry. He had worked for Tunstall. Billy liked and respected the man. Over the months, Tunstall and the Kid had become friends.

Billy hated losing his good friend. He wanted to get back at the killers. The Kid made a promise to himself. He would kill Tunstall's murderers. It was a promise that would change his life.

4

The Lincoln County Wars

Billy the Kid wanted justice for Tunstall. He was not the only one. Others felt the same way. They could not turn to the law. Most of the local lawmen and judges were controlled by Dolan and Murphy.

So, the Kid and his men handled things themselves. They knew a justice of the peace who had liked Tunstall. He made Billy and the other men deputies. Then, they began their hunt for Tunstall's killers. That was the start of the Lincoln County Wars.

The young men fighting for Tunstall became known as Regulators. Billy and the other Regulators tracked down the two killers. They told the men that they were deputies now.

They would only take them to court. That was a lie. Billy and another Regulator shot the men on the way there.

They were not done. The Regulators also wanted to get Sheriff Brady. He had led the deputies who murdered Tunstall. The men planned a surprise attack. The Regulators hid behind some buildings until the Sheriff left the courthouse. Sheriff Brady came out with two deputies. But that did not stop the Regulators. They were ready to take on all three. Within seconds, bullets began flying.

The Sheriff was hit. He died on the spot. The Regulators shot one of the deputies as well.

Here, a cowboy forces a train passenger to drink whiskey. Another makes a man buy pecans at gunpoint.

Western towns were filled with activity. However, if there was a gunfight in the street, the citizens stayed inside.

However, the third deputy was a quick draw. He shot Billy in the leg. The Kid dragged himself to safety. Billy lived and his wound quickly healed.

Billy knew that there was more to do. McSween planned an important battle for June 18, 1878. At least sixty Regulators took part. Some positioned themselves in McSween's

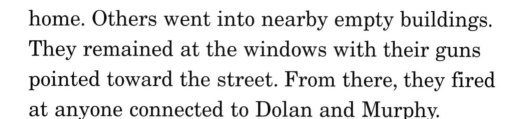

home. Others went into nearby empty buildings. They remained at the windows with their guns pointed toward the street. From there, they fired at anyone connected to Dolan and Murphy.

Their enemies fought back. Dolan and Murphy placed men in other empty buildings. They fired at any Regulator who stepped into the open.

The fighting lasted three days. The town was a mess. Many of the buildings were badly shot up. Businesses had to close. No one wanted to walk down the street during a gunfight.

The United States Army was called in. But the unit that arrived was led by Colonel Nathan Dudley. He was a close friend of James J. Dolan. Dudley wanted to defeat the Regulators. He brought in several cannons. These could do a lot more damage than rifles. Yet, the Regulators did not give up.

The soldiers went even further. They set fire to McSween's house. A large number of Regulators was still inside. Billy was among them. As he and the others ran out, soldiers shot at them. Billy got away, but McSween was killed.

That was the last battle of the Lincoln County War. Things changed with McSween gone. The Regulators lacked leadership. Dolan and Murphy were ready to stop fighting, as well. They had hired men to fight for them. Now they were nearly out of cash.

However, Billy was not ready to quit. With both McSween and Tunstall dead, he felt angrier than ever. Billy and some other Regulators stayed on in Lincoln for a while. At times, they threatened Dolan. They continued to fight with his men. There were several shoot-outs.

But by 1879, the Kid no longer wanted to fight. He was tired of seeing people die. Billy let Dolan's men know it was finally over.

Sometimes, Billy talked with his friends. He told them his plans and dreams. The Kid had spoken about buying a small farm. He felt ready to settle down. But by then, that was impossible. Billy the Kid had become a well-known outlaw who was wanted for some serious crimes. He would never have a peaceful life.

Running From the Law

Billy the Kid remained on the run. He did not have a choice. The law was after him. However, the Kid had a plan to change things. It involved Lew Wallace, the new territorial governor of New Mexico.

Wallace hoped to keep Lincoln County peaceful. He offered full pardons to many who had taken part in the Lincoln County Wars. Wallace promised only to go after the men who had killed people. He wanted them to hang.

That meant trouble for Billy. He had killed a number of people. One had even been a sheriff. Billy wanted to make a deal with Wallace. The Kid had learned that James J. Dolan and one of his men were on trial for

Lew Wallace was a veteran of the Civil War who was originally from Indiana.

murder. Wallace hoped the pair would be found guilty. That seemed unlikely, though. Everyone thought that no one had seen the men commit the crime. So, the case against them was weak.

However, Billy had seen everything. He wrote to Wallace telling him so. Billy offered to tell what he saw in court. In return, he wanted a full pardon. Wallace agreed to the deal.

Billy the Kid did his part at the trial, but he was betrayed. He was not pardoned. Instead, he was arrested for the murder of Sheriff William Brady.

As in the past, Billy did not want to stand trial. He knew he would be found guilty. He was sure he

would hang before his twenty-first birthday.
It had always been hard to keep the Kid jailed.
This time was no different. Billy escaped again.

Wallace was furious. People said
that the Kid had outsmarted him.
Wallace was determined to bring
him back. He offered a $500 reward
for the capture of Billy the Kid.
This was a lot of money in those days.

People who committed murder were sent to gallows to hang.

Meanwhile, Billy hid out near Fort Sumner, New Mexico. The Kid had been there before. Many other outlaws were there too. It was a good place to hide out.

But it was not good enough. Wallace hated looking like a fool. Billy's escape had been embarrassing. Wallace also heard that Billy had been busy lately. He and other outlaws near Fort Sumner were stealing horses again. Wallace vowed to stop the Kid.

In 1880, a new Lincoln County sheriff was elected. He was unusually tall and an excellent shot. His name was Pat Garrett. Wallace ordered Garrett to bring the Kid in. He told him not to waste any time doing it.

Billy the Kid was no stranger to Garrett. They knew each other. Before becoming sheriff, Garrett had been a bartender in a Fort Sumner saloon. That was where he met the Kid. The two had gotten along well. Nevertheless, Garrett had a job to do. He was determined to bring Billy in.

Garrett rode up to Fort Sumner with some deputies. He tried to find out where Billy was

Pat Garrett (center) wanted to catch Billy the Kid and bring him to trial. With Garrett are fellow lawmen James Brent and John Pol.

hiding. No one would tell him anything. Many people in Fort Sumner liked Billy. Others were afraid of the Kid.

Garrett still tracked Billy down. He found him during a snowstorm. Billy and some other outlaws had been out stealing horses. They needed shelter from the storm. So they went to a nearby cabin.

Garrett knew about the cabin. He thought that Billy might be there. He and his men surrounded it. Billy and the others did not know that they had come. They found out when one of the outlaws stepped outside. A deputy shot him.

Garrett called to Billy and the others. He told them to come out. At first, the outlaws refused. But as the hours passed, they changed their minds. There was no heat or food in the cabin. The men grew cold and hungry. One by one, they walked out with their hands up. Billy came out last.

The Kid finally stood trial for Sheriff Brady's murder. He was found guilty and sentenced to die. Billy was to hang two weeks from his date of sentence. In the meantime, he remained behind bars in the Lincoln County Courthouse jail. By now, Billy's jailbreaks were well known. Two guards were ordered to watch him. The Kid remained in handcuffs.

That did not stop Billy. On April 28, 1881, he escaped. Billy had waited until one of the

guards took him to the outdoor toilet. A friend had left a gun for him there. Billy slipped his small hands out of the cuffs. He had a way of bending his thumbs to make his fists smaller. Then, Billy used the gun to kill the guard.

Cabins like this one were not good places to spend cold, snowy days.

The other guard had been having lunch across the street. When he heard the shot, he

Billy was kept here, at the Lincoln County Courthouse, to await his hanging. But once again, he escaped.

ran out of the restaurant. The Kid saw him coming and shot him, too.

Moments later, Billy jumped on a horse and rode off. The townspeople were shocked by what they had seen. No one tried to stop the escaping outlaw. Billy the Kid had cheated the hangman.

The Final Days

Billy the Kid returned to the Fort Sumner area. He had friends there who would hide him. As before, Pat Garrett went after him.

On the night of July 14, 1881, Garrett and his men rode out to Pete Maxwell's ranch. The ranch was near Fort Sumner. Garrett went there for a reason. He came to ask Maxwell if he knew where Billy was.

Garrett had no idea how close he was to Billy. The Kid had been hiding at Maxwell's ranch. While Garrett was talking to Maxwell, Billy had come up to the house. He had a large knife with him. Billy did not bring the knife to harm Garrett. He did not even know that

Billy the Kid and Pat Garrett met for the final time in Pete Maxwell's bedroom, where Garrett shot Billy.

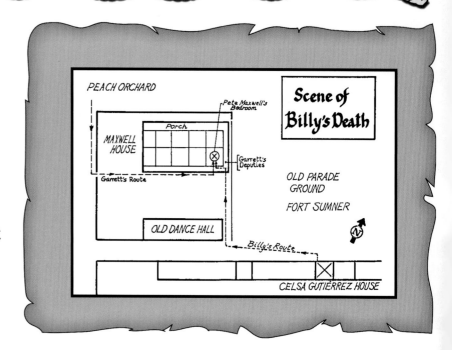

Garrett was there. Billy was just hungry. He had wanted to cut a piece off a side of beef in the kitchen.

That was when it happened. Garrett had been about to leave when he saw Billy. Though the room was dark, he knew it was the Kid. This time, the Sheriff did not try to bring Billy in. Garrett drew his gun and fired. The bullet landed near Billy's heart. At just twenty-one years of age, the Kid was dead.

Pat Garrett, The Man Who Killed Billy the Kid

Pat Garrett was born in 1850 in Chambers County, Alabama. Before coming to New Mexico, he lived in Texas. There, Garrett had been a cowboy and a rancher.

Sheriff Garrett became known for killing Billy the Kid. A bullet later took Garrett's life, as well.

Garrett was shot by a New Mexico rancher in 1908. The sheriff had been involved in a land dispute. Garrett's killer said he had shot in self-defense. However, most people believed the sheriff was murdered.

Billy the Kid was gone but his legend lived on. People liked to tell stories about him. There have been many books and movies about Billy the Kid. Often, these did not tell the whole truth about Billy. Some only stressed Billy's good points. They made him look like a hero. He was not a hero. Billy the Kid was a thief and a killer.

Other times, only the bad things about Billy were stressed. It was said that he killed twenty-one men— one for every year of his life. But this

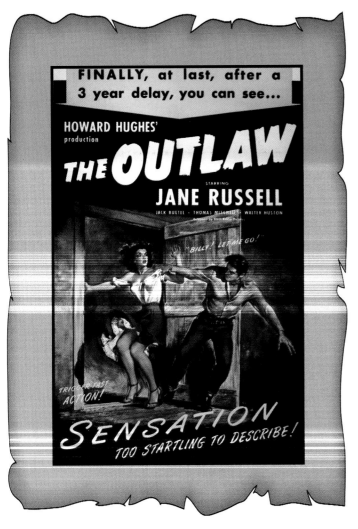

Billy the Kid's short but dramatic life has inspired many movies, such as *The Outlaw*, which came out in 1943.

Barely a month after Billy the Kid was shot, the story of his life was already being told.

is not true, either. Billy killed between seven and nine men.

Many writers felt that Billy was a good subject. He was an outlaw who looked like a boy. That made him special. He also had a charming personality. Yet Billy spent most of his time running from the law.

It is unlikely that the Kid will be forgotten soon. Today, he is known all around the world. Billy the Kid has his own place in the history of America's West.

Timeline

1859—Billy the Kid is probably born on November 23.

1875—Fifteen-year-old Billy makes his first jailbreak.

1877—Billy shoots Windy Cahill. Cahill is the first man to be killed by Billy the Kid.

1878—Billy's boss and friend, John Tunstall, is killed on February 8. His death sparks the start of the Lincoln County Wars.

1878—Alexander McSween is killed on June 18 in the last major battle of the Lincoln County Wars.

1879—Billy the Kid tries to make peace with his enemies in Lincoln County.

1880—Pat Garrett becomes sheriff of Lincoln County. He is given the task of capturing Billy the Kid.

1881—Billy is tried and convicted for Sheriff William Brady's murder.

1881—Pat Garrett kills Billy the Kid on July 14.

Words to Know

bandit—An outlaw or robber who uses a weapon to steal from others.

blacksmith—A person who makes horseshoes and other goods out of iron.

cavalry—A group of soldiers fighting on horseback.

dispute—A disagreement.

dry goods—Material, clothing, and other similar items.

justice of the peace—A type of judge.

merchant—A person who sells goods.

outlaw—A criminal who runs or hides to escape punishment.

pardon—To excuse someone from punishment.

rustlers—Horse thieves.

tuberculosis—A disease of the lungs.

Reading About Billy the Kid

Collins, James L. *Lawmen of the Old West*. Danbury, Conn.: Franklin Watts, 1990.

Glass, Andrew. *Bad Guys: True Stories of Legendary Gunslingers*. New York: Doubleday Books, 1998.

Hamilton, David. *Eyewitness: Cowboy*. New York: DK Publishing, 2000.

Hamilton, John. *Billy the Kid*. Minneapolis, Minn.: Abdo Publishing, 1996.

Harmon, Daniel E. *Billy the Kid*. Broomall, Penn.: Chelsea House, 2002.

Murray, Stuart. *Eyewitness: Wild West*. New York: DK Publishing, 2001.

Internet Addresses

Museum of New Mexico

Visit the Museum of New Mexico's Web site. You will see what the area was like when Billy the Kid lived there.

<http://www.museumofnewmexico.org>

Southern New Mexico Online

Read about the young outlaw who captured headlines throughout the Wild West.

<http://www.southernnewmexico.com/
Articles/Southeast/De_Baca/
FortSumner/TheMysteryof
BillytheKid.html>

Index